Contents

(Numbers in text refer to map)

GW00690730

Introduction

' ...if this Book comes into the hands of gross unbelievers, the account of Apparitions contained in it will be a matter of ridicule to them, who from a certain kind of pride affectedly run down accounts of Apparitions. But is it not an unreasonable kind of unbelief which belies the testimony, and experience, of millions of Men in the World?'

Rev. Edmund Jones, 1779

'To this day people are prone to scoff at 'fairy stories' and 'old wives' tales', but the knowledge of 'The fitness of names' - the Lore of places, their names and the legends associated with them - has always held an important place in the culture of the Celtic peoples. These are an indelible record not only of its own history but also of the character and beliefs of generations of its inhabitants. Our folklore is a part of our common inheritance, without it we are divorced not only from the past but also from our own surroundings.'

G. Burchell, 1989

This booklet is an attempt to restore a small part of their rich cultural heritage to the people of Blaenau Gwent.

1. Ghosts and Apparitions

Tales of the supernatural abound within Blaenau Gwent and few of its towns do not hide a ghostly secret.

Some apparitions were reputedly seen throughout the length and breadth of the Borough - in the 18th century many people were struck with foreboding at the sight of 'corpse candles' in the night air. These were a well known warning of an imminent death.

Tredegar Terrors

The most westerly manifestations in Blaenau Gwent hail from Tredegar. (1) In recent years, people have reported seeing ghosts at Bedwellty House, whilst in 1943 at the Old Cottage Hospital (2) (just west of Bedwellty Park) patients and staff were seized with terror at seeing the ghost of a hook-nosed nun.

The Ebbw Fawr Ghost Trail

Without doubt the dubious honour of 'most haunted' valley in the Borough must be bestowed upon the Ebbw Fawr - stretching from Beaufort in the north down to Aberbeeg in the south.

Poltergeists

(3) During February, 1924, the Meyrick family, who lived on the outskirts of Beaufort were terrorised by a poltergeist ...strange knockings and groans were heard and furniture was seen to move of its own accord. Amazingly, the eerie phenomena ceased almost as suddenly as they had begun.

(4) In 1936, the Jones family were driven from their cottage near Waunlwyd by a heavy 'dark' presence which gave them no rest and even tried to tear the clothes from their bed!

The Berlei Ghost

(5) More recently (1985) strange sounds and lights were reported at night, coming from the former Berlei factory in Ebbw Vale. At Christmas that year, the decorations were torn from the walls, yet there was no trace of how anyone or anything had got into the locked building.

The Betrayed Maiden

(6) Many sightings have been made of the ghost of a young mother and her babe-in-arms walking along the mill stream towards St. John's Church, Ebbw Vale. A local legend explains that the woman had fallen in love with a man considered to be above her station.

At first he returned her love, however, his father wanted him to marry a sea captain's daughter. Soon, the young man's feelings were reduced to mere lust, but the woman would not succumb to his desires until they were married. The young man craftily arranged a false wedding, and the maiden was taken in completely. Not suprisingly, he swore her to a pledge of secrecy.

It was not long before he tired of her, and began to mistreat her until one day he told her their relationship was over. He did not know, however, that she was carrying his child. When the baby was born, the woman's father went to the young man's house. In time he admitted to the illegal marriage and the father begged him to do the honourable thing, but he refused. As a result, the father put a curse on him.

Just before the man's marriage to the captain's daughter the young woman took the child to see him. She and the baby were never seen alive again. They were found drowned in the mill stream.

To this day, no-one knows if in despair she committed suicide or, more gruesomely, if she and the baby were murdered. However, the curse laid upon the young man soon took force - the faithless lover was drowned at sea, leaving his new wife and child as bereft as the woman he had abandoned.

Farm Phantoms
In the 18th Century, two stories were recorded about nearby farms - at Tor-y-Crug, (7) on Mynydd Carn-y-Cefn and Troedrhiwclawdd (8) on the opposite side of the valley. At Tor-y-Crug, a huge black dog haunted a barn where a farmer had committed suicide. Perhaps it was the same spectral hound that terrified Thomas Miles Harry near that spot in the 18th century. Troedrhiwclawdd was haunted by the ghost of a farmer whose body had been salted by his wife and kept in a large chest until heavy snows cleared, allowing him to be buried. The hauntings stopped in 1863 when the farm was renovated and rebuilt. (9) Also in the 18th Century, Walter John Harry of Ty'n-y-Fyd Farm (near Waunlwyd) was haunted by the ghost of the previous owner, Morgan Lewis (a weaver by trade) until, tiring of his nocturnal guest, he admonished him 'I charge thee Morgan Lewis in the name of God that thou trouble my house no more'. The ghost was never seen again!

The stretch of road from Cwm to Aberbeeg has experienced many ghostly sightings.

Sky Dogs
(10) In the 18th Century, one Thomas Andrew was unfortunate enough to meet the Cŵn Wybr (Sky Dogs) or Cŵn Annwn (The Hounds of Hell). These were a pack of dogs led out at night by the King of the Underworld to hunt the souls of the damned. The story's chronicler reports 'I have heard say that these Spiritual Hunting Dogs have been heard to pass by the eaves of several houses before the death of someone in the family'.

P.C. Pope
(11) Since the 1950s a tall cloaked figure has been seen walking along this same stretch of road before disappearing without trace. Is this the ghost of P.C. Hosea Pope killed in a brawl at Aberbeeg in 1911? Does his spirit still patrol his old beat?

The Vanishing Gentleman
(12) In 1980 near the site of the Hanbury Hotel, a local man met a figure in a top hat, who stared him square in the face before pulling out his pocket-watch. Suddenly, a woman's screams rang out from the woods near the site of the Brondeg Filling Station. The figure walked up to the road glancing in the direction they came from. Overcoming his understandable fear, the local man followed on behind until, near a place called the Rhiw, the figure in the top hat vanished.

The Crumlin Ghost
In 1851 the local press was filled with the news of 'the Crumlin Ghost' (13). The stories read that a man had been haunted by the spectre of his recently deceased friend. One bleak and snowy night, the ghost forced the man to follow him through the darkness until they reached a huge boulder. Lifting the stone as if it were a feather, the man found a mattock hidden beneath. The ghost immediately ordered him to throw it into the river, upon which the apparition of his friend disappeared and the poor man went mad - never to recover his wits.

Manmoel U.F.O.
(14) On 25th November, 1975 a more space-age manifestation was sighted by three men travelling home from work. As they drove from Manmoel they saw a bright, flashing light above Rhiw Hill. The glow then flew eastwards at an incredible speed. Was this a U.F.O.?

Ghosts of Gilwern
If the Ebbw Fawr Valley is the Borough's 'most haunted' area, Gilwern and Clydach must surely come a close second .....

(15) Tŷ Gwyn farm (built in the 1600s) is home to a shoulder tapping, sweet smelling poltergeist, while the road to Pwll Du near Tyle Farm (16) has a 17th century ghost with a habit of terrifying large dogs out of their skins!

The Long Man
Nearby, at the site of Bedd-y-Dyn-Hir (17) (the Long Man's Grave), two women on a visit from America in 1903 saw the ghost of the giant himself standing in the road. Another version of the story says the ghost is that of the husband of one of the ladies, who refused to go to America and died of a broken heart when she left him. In times gone by, the whole area was terrorised by a ghost tall enough to look through bedroom windows (the giant again?) and on Hallowe'en, 'ghost night', local people were extremely loath to leave their houses after dark. (See also 'Legends')

The Raven Haired Lady
The Bridgend Inn at Gilwern (18) is said to have a ghost ....A beautiful black haired lady who sits at the foot of the bed in the guestroom.

Faithful Friend
In the graveyard of Llanelli church, (19) on the hill above Gilwern village, there is a carving of a white dog who refused to leave his master's grave, and so froze to death. The dog was buried on the spot. As recently as this century, the statue has been seen to come to life, and his ghost has terrified local poachers on their way home through the graveyard with their ill-gotten gains!

Clydach Gorge
The Saleyard Bridge (20) is said to be haunted by a headless horseman and a disappearing walker; while at Cwm Siôn Matthew, (21) on the opposite side of the Gorge, another of the 'Hounds of Hell' has been seen.

The Old Hag of the Mountains
Finally, a warning to walkers on the hills above (22) Blaina, Abertillery and Brynithel. Beware of the spirit of Juan White, a local witch! 'The apparition has the resemblance of a poor old woman, with an oblong four cornered hat, ash-coloured clothes ....with a pot or wooden can in her hand ...' When not terrifying local people with her hideous screams or cries of 'Wow Up!' her chief delight is leading travellers astray across the hills in misty weather. In the 18th Century, John ap John from Cwmcelyn was so terrified by her (and the sound of her phantom carriage) that he hid his face in the heather until she had passed by! She was seen regularly right up until the 1850s.

2. Fairies

When the Rev. Edmund Jones wrote his invaluable account of the life-style and beliefs of the inhabitants of the old parish of Aberystruth in 1779, he included a chapter on 'Apparitions and Agencies of the Fairies'. The 'Agents of Hell' were not some quaint eccentricity but a fact of daily life to the inhabitants of the day.

The fairies were known to the people of Blaenau Gwent as Bendith eu Mamau ie. 'Their Mothers' Blessing' or alternatively as Y Tylwyth Teg yn y Coed and seemed especially fond of the Female Oak, which was known in the area as Y Brenin Bren 'The King Tree'. It was considered very foolish to harm a female oak tree, for the fairies were sure to take their revenge. If a man was unfortunate enough to offend the fairies he could pay dearly, for they were 'implacable in their resentments, hurting many ....' It was said that they could hear anything that was spoken out of doors, however low the speaker's voice.

A Fear of Fairies
In bad weather, the fairies often sought shelter in people's houses:

> 'and the poor ignorant people, for fear of them, made them welcome by providing clean water in the house; taking care that no knife was near the fire, or other iron instruments, such as they knew were offensive to them, were left in the corner near the fire; ....some were afraid to enter their Gardens by night;' (f).

Two brothers who worked a farm at Cwmcelyn (1) had serious overcrowding problems! One night, one of the brothers:

> ' ....Became very thirsty, and rose up, to come down for a drink. When his brother heard him coming downstairs, he said to him 'Be Cautious, for the House is full of them;' The other being a man of courage answered, 'I don't care who is there, I will have drink,' and his brother, from the Chamber, saw the dancing fairies opening to give him way, both to go and return (g).

Changelings
The greatest fear of the parishioners of the area was that the fairies would steal their babies, leaving changelings in their place 'such as were of no growth, good appearance, or sense'. A baby in the care of 'Dazzy' the wife of Abel Walter of Ebwy Vawr (2) was once lifted out of bed and onto the boards above.* Jennet Francis, (3) of the same valley, actually fought with an unseen force which tried to tear her infant son from her arms, but, as she put it, 'God and me were too hard for him'.

*Cae Dazzy (Dazzy's Field) once stood near Newtown, Ebbw Vale.

The tradition of changelings was an attempt to explain the birth of physically or mentally handicapped children. Perhaps the saddest of Edmund Jones' anecdotes concerns a 'changeling' near Blaina (4).

'But these evil spirits of eternity, unhappily prevailed to change a son of Edmund John William, of the Church Valley to the great trouble of his parents, leaving an Ideot (sic) in his stead. He lived longer than such children used to live, till he was, I think ten or twelve years of age, I saw him myself. There was something diabolical in his aspect, but more of this in his motion and voice; For his motions were mad, and he made very disagreeable screaming sounds, which frightened some strangers who passed by; but I remember not to have heard of any other hurt he did. His complexion was a dark tawny colour. I heard of no changeling in Aberystruth Parish besides.'(h).

Dancing Companies
The fairies had several ways of appearing to men, often they were seen in the guise of 'dancing Companies and Music'.:

'When they appeared like dancing Companies they were desirous to entice persons into their Company, and some were drawn among them and remained among them some time; usually a whole year; as did Edmund William Rees, a Man whom I well knew, and was a Neighbour, who came back at the years end, and looked very bad.'

According to the Rev. Jones, they were fond of 'dry, lightsome places' and their favourite haunts were Hafod-y-Dafal (5) and Cefn Bach near Aberbeeg. It was at Cae'r Cefn near here that he saw, as a child, 'a fairy fold full of a great company', with musicians, and, perhaps, the Fairy Queen herself: (a)

'I well remember the resemblance of a fair woman with a high crown Hat, and a red Jacket, who made a better appearance than the rest, and whom I think they seemed to honour ...' (b).

Legendmongers also have it that on moonlit nights local people used to watch the fairies dance behind Black Cat's Row on Twyn Wenallt, (6) and in the early 1960s Canon Parry-Jones of Llanelli Church found a fairy circle in the field behind the houses (7). At one of the waterfalls further up the Clydach Gorge known as the Rainbow Fall, (8) children used to gather to watch the fairies dance behind the cascading water.

Funerals

When not dancing, the fairies very often appeared like a funeral procession. (9) Once, when he saw such a procession near Aberbeeg, Issac William Thomas of Hafod-y-Dafal:

> ' ....reached his hand and took off the black veil which was over the Bier, and carried it home with him ....I knew the Man myself, and in my youthful days conversed with him several times' (c).

And a similar apparition was seen at Blaina Church (10):

> ' ....Mr. Howell Prosser Curate of Aberystruth seeing a Funeral going down the Church Lane, late in the evening, towards the Church, ...put on his Band (the sign of his authority) in order to go to perform the burial office; and hastened to go to meet the funeral; and when he came to it ....putting his hand to the Bier to help to carry the Corpse, in a moment all vanished; and to his very great surprise and astonishment, there was nothing in his hand but the Skull of a dead Horse.' (d)

Others, namely Edmund Daniel of the Arael Farm (11) saw the fairies flying from mountain top to mountain, most often across Cwm Beeg from Cefn Bach towards Hafod-y-Dafal:

> ' ....leaping and frisking in the air, making a path in the air, much of this form' (e).

Henry Edmund and the Fairy Folk

The fairies were also known to entice people away into the night and were capable of carrying grown men long distances across country. Henry Edmund of Hafod-y-Dafal was once carried from Llanhilleth (12) to a tavern in Llandovery, and back again, in one night! A similar adventure befell Edmund Jones' elder brother in 1733, and the story he tells is such a remarkable one that it deserves repeating in full:

'Mr Edmund Miles of Ty yn yr Llwyn (13) (Tŷ Llwyn) in Ebwy-vawr (Ebbw Vale), and some young men of the neighbourhood, going with him a hunting, to Llangattock Crickhowell, in Breconshire; Mr. Miles having, besides two or three Estates in Ebwy-vawr Valley an Estate in those parts. Among others a brother of mine went with him, Mr. Miles being my father's Landlord. After hunting a great part of the day, and they had sat down to rest, when they were concluding to return home, up started a hare just by them. After which the hounds ran, and they, ran after the hounds. After the hare had given them a long chase, the hounds followed it to the cellar window of Richard the Tailor, who kept the public house in the village of Llangattock, and challenged the hare at the cellar window: that village at that time being very infamous for witches in all the country round, and this man among the rest was believed to be one, and one who resorted to the company of fairies. This begat a suspicion in the company that he was the hare which had played them that trick; to make it too late for them to return home, that they might stay to spend money at his house that night. It being now too late to return home, and being weary, they did stay there. But they were very free in their suspicions and reflections upon him. Mr. Miles who was a sober wise gentleman, altho' of a few words, was not without his suspicion, with the rest, though he persuaded them to speak less. And when my brother, some time in the night, wanted to go out to make water, Mr. Miles, and others with him, dissuaded him from going out, but to do it in the house; which he disdaining to do, ventured to go out; but did not return; which after waiting a while, the company became uneasy, and very stormy, and abusive in Language to the man of the house; threatening to burn the house if my brother did not return, and so troublesome they were, that the man and his wife left the room, and went to bed. The company were still waiting, and expecting his return, and slept little. Next morning, not very early, he came to them. They were exceedingly glad to see him, tho' he appeared like one who had been drawn thro' thorns and briars, with his hair disordered and looking bad, who was naturally a stout man, and of a good healthy complexion. They were very curious to know where he was, until early that day, he saw himself at Twyn Gwnlliw, near the entrance into Newport town, where he helped a man, from Risca, to raise a load of coal which had fallen from his horse. Suddenly after he became insensible, and was brought back into the place from whence he had been taken. In a few hours therefore he must have been carried, by these infernal spirits thro' the air, more than twenty miles, for so long the way is from Newport to Llangattock Village ...After this he became sober and penitent' (i).

The Tasseled Cushion

The fairies were active in other parts of the Borough at varying times. Rees John Rosser of Hendy Farm (14) near Llanhilleth was feeding the oxen early one morning when he decided to lie down in the hay and rest. All of a sudden, he heard the sound of music approaching, and saw a large company dressed in striped clothes enter the barn. The fairies (for that is who they were) began to dance, and Rees watched as silently as he could until a woman, better dressed than the others, brought him a striped cushion with four tassles to rest his head. Suddenly a cockerel crowed at Blaen-y-Cwm Farm across the mountain above Hafodyrynys, and the fairies promptly fled - taking their cushion with them!

'Pwca'

One well travelled sprite was Pwca'r Trwyn a hobgoblin generally associated with Trwyn Farm near Abercarn. He worked for the farmer, until, insulted by one of the maids, he refused to work there anymore and became malicious and mischievous. It is said that he haunted Tŷ Trist (15) ('Sad House') in Tredegar so badly that no-one would live there. His travels took him as far as the forested area near Devil's Bridge, which was once known as Cwm Pwca (Puck's Valley) (16). His magic was so feared that in the 18th century locals used water from Ffynnon Gistfaen as a charm against him. He may also have been active in Nantyglo, for about half a mile north-west of Winchestown is Tŷ Pwca ('Puck's House') (17).

Annelly's Gold

Llanelli and Gilwern have all had their share of fairy stories too! There once was a local man called Annelly, who coming home one night from Blaenafon to Llanelli, met a small, strange man near Gilwern (18) who asked him to carry his bundle. This Annelly did, offering the traveller a bed for the night into the bargain. As a reward, the little man (who was really one of the fairies) took Annelly to one of the many caves in the area and showed him a secret chamber full of gold. Annelly was told that he could come to the cave once a week and take as much gold as he could carry in his mouth. One day, however, Annelly was overcome by greed and stuffed his pockets full. The fairy-man flew into a terrible rage and almost threw Annelly down a ravine, (perhaps into the River Clydach?), and he lost all his gold into the bargain.

3. Local Legends

Battles

Blaenau Gwent has a rich and colourful folklore tradition. Being a fiery people by nature, local legends of a battle fought between the Welsh and the Normans at Trefil (1) are longlived and persistent. Some say that Trefil Ddu and Trefil Las are named after the armies ('the black three thousand' and 'the green three thousand') who are said to have assembled at the farms of Purgad and Hirgan (the latter was also a local centre for prize fighting in the early 19th century). At Rhyd y Milwr (Warrior's Ford) people used to point out the holes in the bed of the stream as the hoof prints of the black army's horses. 'Pwll y Duon' (The Blacks' Pool) is nearby. Local place names certainly seem to suggest a battle field - Troed y Milwyr (the Warriors' Tread), Maes y Beddau (2) (The Field of Graves) and the old stories may contain an echo of an actual battle fought somewhere in the area which is recorded in the medieval Welsh Chronicles. Some people claim that the name Sirhowy comes from the answer given to the Welsh general by his men when he asked who was willing to fight for him: 'Syr wy i' - 'Sir, I am' (3). In 1850, Dr. William Price - the eccentric physician from Llantrisant held an open air congress of bards to honour the site of the battle.

Romans!

Local tradition also claim Clwyd y Sarn 'The Paved Way Gate' (4) (near the Mountain Air), Y Sarnm Hir 'The Long Paved Way' (5) (on Bedwellty Mountain), and y Ffordd Rhufeinig 'The Roman Road' (6) (from Rhymney through Dukestown) as Roman Roads, and Archdeacon Coxe in 1801 stated that the area at the rear of St. Illtyd's Church known as Castell Taliorum was of Roman origin as he took Taliorum to be a corruption of Italiorum from the latin 'of the Romans'.

Wil Eight Tune

To the north of the Mountain Air gate is a strange outcrop of rock which local people in the 1930s still called Bedd Wil Wyth Tiwn (Wil Eight Tune's Grave) (7) - Wil was a fiddler who, it is said, could play only eight tunes and who committed suicide.

The Lamb Stone

In the 1770's a standing stone at Bwlch y Llwyn (8) on the Milfraen Mountain above Nantyglo stood as a marker for travellers from Abergavenny. A small stone at its base was reputed to carry the miraculous print of a young lamb's foot.

Blaina Church

From the same source comes the tale of how Blaina Church (9) came to be built where it was. The parishioners could not decide where to build the church, some favouring a spot called Lle'r Eglwys (Church Place) on top of Mynydd Carn y Cefn, and others a place above Abertillery called Ty Llawn Bwn march (The House of the full-loaded Horse) (10) - 'where they say was a print of the Horse's foot upon a Stone to be seen formerly, which had brought there a load of Money to build a Church in that place'. Finally the parishioners decided to build the church in Blaina, where its modern replacement now stands. Another version of the story says that after the horse returned to its master (the Devil!) in a ball of flame, the parishioners were led to the 'correct' site by a strange floating light!

Tales of St. Illtyd's

Many myths surround the 12th century church of St. Illtyd, and the immediate landscape. One story claims that at Llanhilleth, there lived a giant called Ithel, who, deciding to build himself a house, started collecting boulders from Cefn Grib above Hafodyrynys (11). As he was carrying them back in his apron, the string broke and he dropped the large stones, creating the mound (12) next to St. Illtyd's church. Legend also has it that the altar of the church (13) was once adorned by a golden calf which was stolen by two thieves. On discovering the loss, the furious parishioners gave chase and caught the culprits in the woods beneath Pen-y-Fan Uchaf Farm (on the other side of the valley). When confronted, they confessed to burying the calf under a white hawthorn tree. The villagers dug up every white hawthorn - in vain - and to this day no white hawthorns grow in those woods.

The Long Man

Gilwern has a store of local legends, the most famous being those attached to Bedd y Dyn Hir (The Long Man's Grave) (14) and Carreg Bica (15) (The Lonely Shepherd). The Long Man's Grave stands on the road from Gilwern to Pwll Du at Twyn Wenallt. According to a story recorded by Edmund Jones, the giant was born at Hafod-y-Dafal near Aberbeeg in the days before the church was built at Blaina. When he died, his friends and relations began carrying his body over the mountains to be buried at Llanwenarth church, in the Usk Valley. Having got as far as Twyn Wenallt, the company were overtaken by a dreadful storm, and, being exhausted by their exertions and having still some way to go, they buried him on the spot. As Edmund Jones says 'He must have been a person of an extra-ordinary size, and certainly a

Giant, and tall as Goliath of Gath' (j). Other sources say he had six fingers on each hand. The story is a very old one because 'Bedd-y-gwr-hir' 'The Long Man's Grave' is mentioned in an Elizabethan document as one of the boundary markers of the old parish of Llanelli. In more recent times, people have reported seeing the Giant's ghost near the site of his grave. (See 'Ghosts and Apparitions').

The Lonely Shepherd

On the opposite side of the Gorge, a thin needle of limestone can be seen on the skyline - this is Carreg Bica, (15) known in English as the Peaky Stone or the Lonely Shepherd. Once, so legend has it, it was a man, the tenant of Tŷ Isaf farm, about a mile below. He was so cruel to his wife that she drowned herself in the River Usk. The farmer, for his sins, was turned to stone, but at midnight on Midsummer's Eve he walks down the hill to the river, calling his wife's name as he goes and trying to persuade her to come back to him. The dawn finds him back on top of the hill. It was the custom among local people to whitewash the stone once a year so that they could see him coming when he walked down through the village!

Cromwell's Cup

Local legends also tell of an old farmhouse at the foot of Gilwern Hill (16) which was visited by Oliver Cromwell and his men during the Civil War.

They were fed on brown bread and milk, and Cromwell's Cup - a small jug from which the great man drank - was preserved in a house in Clydach until the end of the last century.

Shakespeare's Cave

The area near Devil's Bridge was named Cwm Pwca after a wicked sprite. It is said that Pwca was the inspiration for Puck in 'A Midsummer Night's Dream'. It is even believed that it was here that Shakespeare wrote his play. In the last century, local people would point out the houses where the Bard was believed to have stayed (Clydach or Aberclydach House). In the narrow ravine east of Lower Fedw Ddu is 'Shakespeare's Cave' (see also 'Fairies') (17). This site is inaccessible and potentially dangerous.

4. Witches and Wizards

Mari Can Punt

The belief in the existence of powerful witches and warlocks was rife amongst the people of Blaenau Gwent. In Ebbw Vale, as late as the 1870's, Mari Can Punt, a straw-seller from Beaufort, (1) was widely believed to be a witch. So was another old woman from Llandafal, near Cwm, (2) who was reputed to be able to concoct potions in her iron cauldron which enabled her to change into a cat or a rabbit at will.

Richard Black Cap

The best recorded instance of witchcraft in the Borough concerns not a witch but a warlock - 'Rissiart Cap Dee' (Richard Black Cap) who lived at the foot of Rhiw Coelbren (3) (somewhere above the Old Blaina Road just south of the Tylers Arms at Bournville). In 1779, the Rev. Edmund Jones wrote of him:

> ' ....there was a large hole in the side of the Thatch of his House, thro' which the people believed he went out, at night to the Fairies, and came in from them at night; but he pretended it was that he might see the stars at night ...He is yet said to be an affable friendly Man and cheerful; 'tis then a pity he should be in alliance with Hell, and an Agent in the Kingdom of Darkness'. (k)

It was said that 'Rissiart Cap Dee' joined the fairies on their nocturnal excursions, and was often seen to join them in injuring his neighbours.

Mari'r Gwrhyd

There was a witch called Mari'r Gwrhyd who lived at Gwrhyd Farm (4) in Cwmtillery. One day she visited Hendre Gwyndir Farm further up the Valley and asked for a small loaf, which the occupant, fearing her reputation, gave her. At home, she found barley as well as wheat flour in the bread and, taking this as an insult, flew into a rage. She obviously put a curse on the cows at Hendre Gwyndir Farm, for despite churning for three days and nights, no butter could be made from their milk. The maids tried to make cakes from the cream, but the dough ran and stuck, and when it was finally fed to the pigs, they fell sick from the effects of the spell.

Old Ann

A woman called Old Ann lived in a hovel at Cwmcelyn (5) and was believed to be possessed by the Devil. If local farmers were foolish enough to refuse her bread, their milk would never churn. A neighbour of hers, called Robert ap Watkin, owned eleven mules, and when he refused her the loan of one of them to collect winter fuel, she bewitched them and they all disappeared. A repentant Robert went to Ann cap-in-hand to be told 'Ewch i'r Ffynhonnau Oerion yng Nghwmtyleri' ('Go to the Cold Springs in Cwmtillery'). Sure enough, the mules were there.

The Penrhiwllech Coven
Halfway up the forest path from Aberbeeg to Hafod-y-Dafal is a barn called Penrhiwllech. (6) Here, at Hallowe'en, a coven of witches and wizards would meet at midnight to ride the horses sheltering in the barn. The animals' terrified screams would keep the entire neighbourhood awake and trembling in their beds.

Healers
Gilwern and the surrounding area (especially Llangenny) was renowned in times past for its 'wise men' or charmers - men who used charms and spells to cure human and animal ailments. The best known was Solomon Chilton of Rhonos Uchaf Farm, (7) who usually wore a tall hat and rode a small pony. For a few pence (or a few pints!), Solomon would cure foul in the foot by removing a turf with the affected animal's hoofprint, mumbling a few mysterious incantations over it, and then placing the turf high in a blackthorn bush. As the clod rotted and disintegrated so did the disease.

Other charmers used spells written on scraps of paper to cure toothache, while at Cwm Nant Gam (8) and Tyle, hernias were cured by passing people three times through a split ash sapling.

The School Sorceress
Molly Davies opened a school in 1794 near the Clydach Ironworks (9). Attendance was exceptionally high and regular, because, as well as being a teacher, local people thought her a witch. She was reputedly able to fly a broomstick, make pigs stand on their heads, and turn milk into ditch-water.

Local Charms
With all these mysterious goings-on, it is hardly suprising that local people had a whole range of charms and talismens to ward off the power of witches and their maledictions. Elder and mountain ash were considered very effective in deflecting evil spells, and on May Eve, sprigs of both would be placed on stable doors to prevent witches riding and ruining the horses. Mountain Ash was planted in front of cottages and carried at night in peoples pockets as a charm against the fairies.

If a person had the misfortune to be placed under a spell, the only way to reverse its effect was to draw blood from the witch who had cast it.

16

5. Customs and Superstitions

The differing seasons of the year and special occasions, such as marriages and funerals, were marked by local customs and ceremonies. Christmas saw the Plygain and Mari Lwyd.

The Plygain

This was an early morning carol service. The candles and altar of the church or chapel would be decorated by the women and girls of the village with ribbons and brightly coloured paper, and especially composed Christmas carols were sung. The custom was thriving in Blaina in 1779 and survived in Ebbw Vale until 1859, with the last recorded Plygain held at Penuel Chapel.

Mari Lwyd

Less directly religious in character was the Mari Lwyd. A horse's skull (or a wooden effigy) was decorated with ribbons and rosettes and carried from house to house on a pole with a sheet covering the bearer. Accompanied by singers and musicians, the Mari Lwyd would knock on the door and an impromptu riddling competition would begin which culminated in the Mari Lwyd being let into the house. After dancing, singing, and chasing after the girls of the household, the whole party would sit down to eat and drink.

At one time the custom was widespread all over Gwent (it was held in 1838 at Govilon) - especially in the Welsh speaking areas of the north and west, but as the Welsh language lost ground so too did the Mari Lwyd. It was extinct in Tredegar by the second half of the 19th century, though it was still thriving in Briery Hill, Beaufort and Gilwern in the 1870s. The last recorded appearance of the Mari Lwyd in the Borough was in the Rassau during the 1880s.

Pastai

Weddings and funerals also had their respective customs and superstitions. In the 19th century at Blaina, Nantyglo, Tredegar and Rhymney, a pastai (PA) was held after the reading of the banns. Pastai is the Welsh word for a pie or pasty, and people were invited to a gathering at a local tavern where they were fed on pie and beer. Each invited couple would bring a gift of money, or clothing, or furniture to help the betrothed couple set up home. In Tredegar, 40 or 50 couples would be invited to the wedding and again, each brought a present. The compliment was to be returned as soon as possible. In Llanelli and Gilwern it was widely considered most unlucky for a man to hear the banns for his own wedding being read.

Should the path of true love not run smooth, people in Tredegar had their own method of dealing with adultery. The guilty parties were forcibly tied to a plank or ladder and, accompanied by a large and derisive crowd, paraded through the streets before being pelted with stones, mud, dung and rotten eggs. This custom continued into the early years of this century.

Choosing The Groom
Before the marriage, of course, there was the question of finding a suitable partner, and young women in Gilwern and Llanelli had a strange ritual for predicting who the lucky man would be, or whether or not there was to be a wedding at all! A large door key was placed on chapter one of the Book of Ruth and the Bible closed and bound up with the garter from the girl's left leg' ...Two girls then put their middle fingers under the key loop to hold the Bible up and if it turned ...while the girls recited, a special verse, it meant the girl would marry the boy she had in mind. If the bible fell ...there would be no marriage'. (1)

Cwrdd-Gweddi
Burying the dead had its own series of customs to be observed. The most longlived was the tradition of *codi'r angladd* or the *cwrdd-gweddi* (CD) ('raising the funeral' or the 'prayer meeting'). Before the funeral, a short service was held at the house of the deceased which was often decorated with white sheets for the purpose. The custom of holding a service at the house is still prevalent in the valley towns of the Borough. People would travel for miles and miles to attend a funeral. At Llanelli Parish Church, the procession would wind up Church Road from the village, in twos, with hymn-singing all the way. Wakes were held after the service in the Five Bells Inn (now a private residence), and many lasted from the Saturday (the favoured day for funerals) to the following Monday, when the revellers' relatives would arrive to drag them off to work. (It was believed impossible for someone to die in a feather bed!)

Llanelli Parish
In 1785, Rev. Henry Thomas Payne wrote an account in his diary of the customs of his parishioners at Llanelli. It was considered a great honour to be buried under the floor of the church rather than in the churchyard. So many people wanted to be buried there that some of the bodies were placed very close to the surface. The result was inevitable! It is reported that a local clergyman 'had oftentimes been obliged to quit the church in the midst of divine service, being quite overcome with the stench from the putrid carcasses'. (m) Another alarming custom was that of the common charnel, 'where the bones of the deceased have been for ages past, piled up in a corner of the churchyard ...and left scattered about to be bandied by boys or, to the disgrace of humanity, to be gnawed by dogs'. (n) This custom was ended by the Rev. Payne who ordered pits dug for the bones to be properly buried.

18

On Palm Sunday, Llanelli's medieval preaching cross was decorated with flowers and garlands as a communal memorial for those buried in unmarked graves. Bargains struck in its shadow were considered particularly binding - woe betide the man who broke them!

Gŵyl Mabsant ('Wake')

This was another facet of local life, and consisted of an open air festival held on the feast day of the patron saint of the parish church. The occasion was celebrated with feasting, drinking, dancing and traditional sports. The feast was held in June at Blaina, and in 1779 Edmund Jones reported disapprovingly that ' ...no devotion of any kind is performed, but abundance of sin committed, for nothing else but sin is the work of the day, and the measure of sinning very great'. At Llanelli Parish church, the feast was held on the Sunday before August 12th. Services were held in the morning, while the rest of the day was given over to traditional sports. There was racing, jumping, putting the weight, wrestling, bando (a sort of Welsh hurling), and even horse-racing. Also, bare-knuckle prize fighting took place, and in 1793 Richard Pritchard, who lived near Clydach House, was so severely beaten in one bout that he died from his injuries. In the evening, the merriment moved to the local tavern where dancing and drinking took up the rest of the night.

Sirhowy

It was customary in this valley for people to gather at each other's houses during the long winter evenings for Welsh Bible readings (BR). They were usually held at Pen Rhos, Llyswedog Fach or Twyn Sirhywi Farms. Glan Rhyd Uchaf (near Dukestown) was a resting place for the drovers, on their way with their cattle from west Wales to the great markets in London, and also a centre for prize fighting. (PF) One of the greatest local exponents of the 'science of pugilism' was John Jones, better known as Sioni Sguborfawr (named after his birthplace on the lower side of the road halfway between Heathfield and Bedwellty Pits), a close friend of the local poet Dai'r Cantwr. Having fled to west Wales from the aftermath of the Chartist Uprising of 1839, they both took part in the Rebecca Riots of 1843 and were transported to Tasmania for 'the term of their natural life'.

Sleeping Swallows

It was formerly believed that rather than migrating in winter, swallows hibernated underground or in caves, and in 1779 'A Man of the Parish who worked at the Coal Mine in Rhase yr Glo ('the coal-races' i.e. the Rassau) ...found there a number of swallows ....in their sleeping state'. (o)

Floral Superstitions

In Gilwern and Llanelli elder wood was never used as fuel because it was believed to be the tree on which Christ was crucified. Snowdrops were never allowed in the house, and if daffodils were taken indoors before Easter, the housewife's goose-eggs would never hatch.

Various other customs are recorded, for instance in the 18th century, low cloud over Y Domen Fawr was taken (not suprisingly) as a sure portent of rain, while later on, when the town of Ebbw Vale was developing, harpists and *baledwyr* ('ballad singers') were a common sight in the town's pubs of a Saturday evening. In Tredegar an annual gathering similar to the *gŵyl mabsant* was held at Y Felin ('The Mill') to the south of the town, whose millstone now rests in Bedwellty Park.

6. Healing Wells

In Celtic countries, a belief in the healing properties of certain wells or springs was widespread. The roots of such a belief lie buried in the distant past, when offerings of gold and weapons, and sometimes human lives, were made to water gods and goddesses believed to live in lakes and wells.

Ffynnon Wen

(The White or Sacred Well), also known as Ffynnon Illtyd (Illtyd's Well) stood near Argoed Farm at Brynithel. People would travel to the well to bathe wounds and sprains in the hope of a cure.

The Ffynhonnau Oerion

(The Cold Springs) give their name to the mountain to the east of Cwmtillery, and were also considered to have healing properties. In the 18th century groups of huntsmen would stop there to slake their thirst.

'Ffynnon Y Rhiw Newyth'

The Rev. Edmund Jones describes another healing well somewhere near Blaina:

' ...the medicinal Well called Ffynnon y Rhiw Newyth, in the Church Valley... It was said to have performed many cures in times past, and had stones put about it by some virtuous benevolent person; but it was demolished by a malevolent drunken man... The Well is now deserted, as if it had lost its virtue, which yet I am not sure it hath, if people tried it in faith and sobriety'. (p)

The Clydach Wells

The Fountain of the Stone Chest 'Ffynnon Gistfaen' and the Cuckoo's Well 'Ffynnon y Gog' in the Clydach Gorge were also believed to have medicinal properties. In the later 1780s the Rev. Henry Thomas Payne described this scene at Ffynnon Gistfaen:

' ...I observed an old woman descending by a dangerously steep path from the summit of the mountain to the dingle. Where it was possible for her to do it with safety, she stopped, and spent a few minutes upon her knees with her hands clasped together, seemingly in fervent prayer. This was repeated several times in the course of the descent.

At length, having reached the bottom, she devoutly crossed herself, knelt down, and seemed to pray with great agitation for about a quarter of an hour. She then took off her shoes and stockings, neck kerchief and cap, walked into the water of the well, and stooping down, threw it backwards over her head. Afterwards she washed her face, neck and head, as well as her feet, and concluded the ceremony by a long prayer upon her knees before she dressed herself'. (g)

There was also a well on the Rhotfa (the angle of land between the River Usk and the River Clydach) which was believed to have miraculous powers.

Notes

a. Jones, Edmund   **A Geographical, Historical and Religious Account of the Parish of Aberystruth, (Trevecka, 1779), p.70**

b. **ibid,** p.76

c. **ibid,** p.74

d. **ibid,** p.73

e. **ibid,** p.75

f. **ibid,** p.77

g. **ibid,** p.79

h. **ibid,** pp.79-80

i. **ibid,** pp.80-82

j. **ibid,** p.64

k. **ibid,** p.70

l. Parry-Jones, D.   'Horses Bewitched, Llanelly Parish, Breconshire', South Wales Argus, April 25, 1963.

m. Parry-Jones, D.   'A Quaint Little Church', **ibid,** May 23, 1963.

n. **ibid,** May 30, 1963.

o. Jones, (1779), p.62

p. **ibid,** pp.18-19

q. Parry-Jones, **op. cit.,** August 15, 1963.

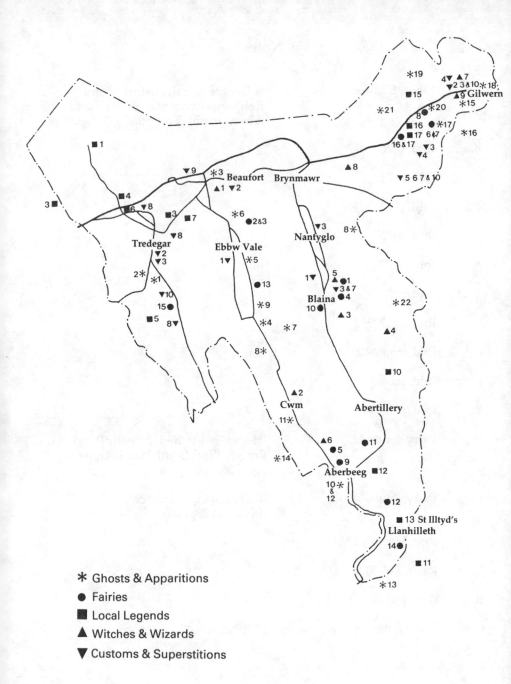

* Ghosts & Apparitions
● Fairies
■ Local Legends
▲ Witches & Wizards
▼ Customs & Superstitions